G878

47126

PLANS FOR AN ORDERLY APOCALYPSE
and Other Poems

PLANS FOR
AN ORDERLY APOCALYPSE

and Other Poems

by Harvey Gross

Ann Arbor
The University of Michigan Press

Str 495/248/3/11/69

ACKNOWLEDGMENTS

Some of these poems appeared in a manuscript given a major Hopwood Award at The University of Michigan (1953). Others have been published as follows:

"The Tapestry" and "Plans for an Orderly Apocalypse" in *Poetry*, October 1953.

"Ruins" in *Western Review*, Summer 1955.

"Final Evening with Dr. Faust" in *The Beloit Poetry Journal*, Spring 1956.

"Grodek" in *Prairie Schooner*, Summer 1963. Copyright 1963 by The University of Nebraska Press.

"Delphi Remembered" and "The Journey to Castalia" in *The Virginia Quarterly Review*, Winter 1966.

I wish to thank the editors of these magazines for permission to reprint my poems here.

My friends James McMichael and X. J. Kennedy have given me invaluable help in preparing this volume.

FOR GINNIE

CONTENTS

PROLOGUE

My demon comes, not when called but when
The shuddering hours kneel down.
Now past and future fade
With noise of ringing metal.
Unknotted, hand and eye recall their love:
In this dark interval I grasp the day.

I have lived from hour to hour, bent
Under the dark, under the night,
Knowing I am the city
In whose stony streets I search
The future with its meager face,
Or face the past, holding didactic talk
With disapproving ghosts.

I greet my benign magician,
Guardian of the double gates:
No smoky angel, not wincing with wounds,
Wise and bright in his garments
Streaming with the rain of his voyage.

He urges his semblance in music.
Incredible graces; with a voice as clear
As spring sunlight when it tests the air!
His song moves against our city,
Dark with dying and the cries of love,
Ringed in sound I listen,
                                        and grow in melody.

On the coldest midnight of the year
Our mouse with frosted whiskers
Struggled in his mousetrap world.
This world, our world,
Went rumbling on its wooden wheels,
Crushing the groaners underneath the city wall.
No bedtime child but cried that night,
No burgher's wife but brought her maid to tears.
Winter thunder shook the house;
Such winds rose up as never raged
Down inlet and island, between house and field,
Rattling in the rooftree, singing in the wires.

I dreamed foul water filtered through the floor;
Wings and talons scratched the windowpanes.
I heard the recent hero of the rack
Learn the light is dark and darkness can't be learned.
Ten devils ground his face in gravel:
This method brought him final health,
Taught him richer knowledge:
The night was deeper than the day had thought.

We live so close upon the world's collapse
That though you have my history intact
(How I gave a Roman mob its miracle;
Amused the Emperor Charles with fireworks)
You credit my conscience to act perfection
On a stage of living days and hours,

2

For a new world and in a better time.
You forget I signed a compact with my blood. . . .

This music brings me to myself. Tonight
I tuned my ringing glass to twelve.
And now our guest arrives,
Extravagant with violins and drums.
This is no cardboard pantomime
Of retort flames and flannel devils;
No wooden apparition
Sent rolling through the echoing wings.
                                        But I recall

Seven days at The Eye of God Hotel;
(The trolleys rattled in the broken street.)
An evening at the Schloss Schonburg
Where foreign eyes dispatched me like a knife.
Under the long cold staircase my familiar waited.

Everyman to his mystery. Our way
Leads upward in a puff of cloud,
While the good work goes on below
With hooks and bills. They prepare our proper beds,
Drawing out our lengths, or lopping off our legs.
We cannot complain:
Fair play is scrupulously practiced.
Before they stretch my skin,
I've wonders to report.
                                        Let me begin.

3

THE TAPESTRY

—*after Stefan George*

Monsters and men are woven in this cloth,
Framed strangely in its silken fringe. They clash
In cold ballet: blue sickles, white stars slash
On head and helmet, unicorn and Goth.

And bald lines run through rich embroidered parts,
And every part is tangled and opposed,
And no one solves the riddle that is posed:
The riddle of the snared man and the beast.

At night the knotted fabric lives and grows.
Dead branches scrape; the shapes confined in ring
And thread step clean before the cloth and bring
The answer to the agony they pose.

This thing is not for ordinary hours;
The image comes but rarely to the rare.
The pattern is not willed, nor do we dare
Invoke its meaning and bewildering powers.

At five o'clock we heard the swinging bell
Ringing us home. We heard the strident yell
And saw the deep swoop of the hungry gull,
Tasting the waste in the ship's wake. The dull
Morning lowered on the wet deck, the day
Prepared for summer heat. The Lower Bay
Churned into sight; the pointed city burst
Against the heated sky. This city, first
Father to the child, stone cradle of hate
And youngest love, and symbol of the state;
Hot with certainty, red with pride and pain,
Stood upright in the rising sun. The stain
Of day spread on the water like a wound—
Blazed from the Jersey shore, and quickly found
The mirrored points of windows. Again the bell,
Riding the oil and backwash, rose and fell
To mark the morning's half-past five:
Time's iron bell, to tell you you're alive.

Like a saint asleep between a landscape and a dream,
In a garden by a cold east light I slept and waited.
The way was green with leaves, tall with the trunks of trees,
Wet with morning rain where God's own shadow
Walked in the shadows by pool and stream and fountain.

I slept and woke and slept again. I dreamed in daylight
The earth faltered, the dragon-feet of the world stumbled and
    clawed,
Old gods growled underground. Sibilant voices tore at silence:
Hoots and catcalls; familiar obscenities; whispers of derision;
Words that turned in the wind . . . echoed, reechoed . . . were lost.

At moonrise I woke in wonder, chill with night frost.
A muffled owl flew; a stiff cat spooked at the rustling leaves;
Flute and drum played nightmare music all night long,
And the ground beat with the feet of leaping lunatics,
Circling the stone in an orbit of power and spite.

The priestess howled above the tripod, tearing her breasts,
Joining word to stumbling word. But what sentence hung in the
    smoke,
What warning whistled in the foggy air—these were not recorded.
Only the noise of men who could not struggle into life,
Only the cries of stricken gods who could not fade in death.

I returned with the god smell still in my nose.
The sun burned on the horizon, shadows lengthened the trees

And crossed the dusty road. I hurried homeward,
Southward toward open water.

                              Memory fades:

Here in the clear light of the humane city,
Where the wind's gentle ardor, the sun's order
Hasten the dogwood in the arbor, and the long days
Hold back the edge of night,

                              I remember

That the garden drowned in winds and gray clouds,
That the willow and the rose tree withered in the fog.

AT THE CROSSROADS

They drove the thorny wood beneath my breast;
The priest's hand trembled and he looked away.
I lie and breathe in sour black earth all day,
In porous earth I lie, awake, unblest.

Dry blood still flecks the corners of my mouth.
The green tree holds me fast; my heart is pinned
Where Cain the furious exile tilled and sinned.
I turn and cry the dumb cry of my drouth.

The live world pounds and rumbles overhead.
Along the crossroads where I died and found
My bed in roots and clay, I strain to hear

The grind of wheel on stone, the sudden tear
Of plow or drill, and water underground.
I smell the beating blood on which I fed.

8

SONG

She sat on the edge of the narrow bed,
With her long hair twisted on the top of her head,
With her white arms folded behind her sweet head,
       —Was it a dream that I dreamed long ago?

She smiled a queer smile that made my blood beat,
Made old Adam ascend with unusual heat,
And the fire went down from my brains to my feet,
       —Was it a dream that I dreamed long ago?

We met in the middle of that narrow bed,
We kissed in the shadows till all shadows fled,
We loved until morning arched over my head,
       —In that dream that I dreamed long ago.

FRAU MIT SCHATTEN

1

Shapes dance in the flicker of morning:
Here and now in the morning,
When the birds cry;
Here and now in the green evening,
When the bats cry.

Again in the night,
In the door of a sleeping house,
A woman struggles against her shadow.
Insistent, he sings:
O my tower, my arbor,
My vineyard,
O beloved!

She flees along the red stones,
Between the trees, standing like green conspirators.
She falls in a doorway, engulfed by her shadow.
The doorway opens to darkness.
Night is cornered; walls restrain
And dissolve in shadow

The blaze of their hands, the mouths of their love.

2

A fish breaks from a green pool,
The cold water ripples,

Ascends like fire
To her breast.

Her heart beats like a bird,
Like a hurt child.
Under her shadow,
Under her lingering shadow,

Lengthening above her,
Quenching her brightness.

3
How may I hold this weather?
The dogwood, the plum tree, the daffodil?
My complaint is with the spring:
Can God repair this weather?
Under the grass the cutworm rustles,
The snail leaks along the youngest leaves.

Restrain all this!
I will hold back the weather,
These stupid months,
The spring!

In the cold hour before the lights go on,
A wind down from the Danube
Cuts the city like a circular saw.
A Christmas crowd huddles along the walls,
Shoves and turns, stares into the lighted shops.
Krampus, our reigning deity and obscene devil,
Leers from the window, fingers his switch,
Scaring naughty boys and soft-rumped girls.

No city so black . . .
Stone laced in soot, the scarred Cathedral
Bulks in the square, cannot ascend,
Squats in its rubble.
Green and yellow tiles catch the winter sun,
Gleam above the Habsburg eagles,
Above a city of writhing men and wounded gods.
Stone heroes clog the squares, invade the parks;
Wingèd furies ride the roofs; hard-breasted caryatids
Gasp beneath facades. Brute Hercules
Defends his twisted gate against the riders
Who charge the empty air.

History hardens. Merging shadows rehearse
The mind's quick show:
Our cousin the Archduke, with his Hungarian moustache
And shattered, bandaged head;
His girl shoved down in frozen mud,
With such maimed rites. . . .

The blood-sick emperors of Rome
Listening for the horns and drums of Rising Day.

Again and now again:
Emerge Lueger, the Jew-hater;
Dollfuss the grinning dwarf, the butcher Fey;
Demented counselors of the sharpened tooth,
Left to bleed behind the Hofburg stairs.
Outrage and rape survive in jokes,
Comic opera revolution,
Bitter heroism at the *Karl Marx Hof,*
A broken mouth on the gallows crying
'*Lebe der Sozialismus, lebe die Freiheit!*'
These ghosts implore in lipless supplication:
Hands that twitch, eyes that curse and kill.

No city so dead . . .
Die alte Frau, die alte Marschallin
Ist . . . ist . . . schon gestorben.
Werdenberg rots: long mirrors reflect
Peeling walls, empty rooms and empty beds.
Down sickening corridors
The past returns upon itself:
Cracked lips to cold image in the cracked glass.
Night moves into the Ring.
Above the church the clouds uncoil,
Dumping snow on every blackened monument.
I move from dark to light, enter a cafe.
Was wünschen Sie, mein Herr? the waiter sneers.

RUINS

—*after Gottfried Benn*

Spook. My brain runs scales all night.
Kiss and claw and with the light
The pale absurdities of day.
Crash. A marble bust
Is stains and dust.
Maréchal Niel the Fair:
Your image rots in the Rathaus Square.

The scattered splinters lie
White against the morning sky.
Simple truth is double now:
You and the infinite.
What more can we allow?
Drink. A thousand ghosts
Rush to hang their lips within your glass.

Aphrodite and the Holy Grail,
Akropolis and Temple fail—
Drowned in the waters of the world.
Spook. Darkness and blood,
A withered wood.
Hear the sick cry out and toss,
In the Ward endowed by Adam's loss.

See the black letters twisted
Behind the grill? Here listed
Are traitors and well-known Jews,
Marked for hand and shame:

14

Death is the same.
Decline. Blown seas and distant wars.
Everything. Suns and poles and stars.

Come, crowd teat to teat,
Take your pleasure naked and neat.
Renounce. In the howling desert.
Spook. Assume the stage:
Oboes squeal, scales rage . . .
The gods decline like rose leaves falling.
Playtime is over; the horns cease calling.

THE WATCHMAN

—after Rilke

Madness is night watchman. He cries the hours,
The numbered names of Night. He laughs
And calls Her: Seven, Eight and Twenty, Ten . . .
The bronze bells strike the quarters and the halves.
On twenty towers
The grinding clocks send out their armored men.

He holds a triangle. It tingles in his hand,
Shivers silver metal on the horn
He cannot blow. And sings
A song that pierces every house and brings
The mandrake, dragged from violated land.

The children sleep secure in their good night,
And hear in dreams that madness keeps the clock.
The dogs, their hackles stiff in fright,
Circle the houses.
Trembling, they hear his footsteps . . . his fumbling knock.

SONG

In April on a day
In a corner of our garden,
We played at Eve and Adam,
      My lady led the way.

Uncoiled all her hair
Unbuttoned down her dress,
Let me, let me confess:
      What wantonness was there!

"I cannot live!" she cried,
And shuddered underneath.
My sword leapt in its sheath
      —And as we moved, we died.

A SUMMER MORNING'S DREAM

Level in the sleeper's eye, a dream
Of a familiar place: Claude and Poussin
Knew these bearded trees, this whisper of water,
These groves rich in suggestion and shadow.
Here the hunter's worried quarry
Rustles in dry leaves, here the lurching spider
Weaves to fracture sunlight in his prism.

Let us linger near the lip of this park.
The well-ordered ruins do not disturb
Symmetry. Shepherd and shepherdess speak
A cultured dialect of no country.
A nymph bends back from her innocent eyes
(Meeting her own gaze in a quiet pool)
To meet the faun's archaic leer,
The centaur's half-extended hoof.

Voices call across the meadow,
Across the landscape of the sleeping head,
Dreaming our father's first bright dream of heaven.
Mask of the driven will! Can we return
To such country, slip under the long sword
Of turning fire? Or only knotted in sleep
Encounter the child's joy, relive the grace
Suspended by the daylight's filching power?

The loss in only seeming, not regret.
The moon's dominion is a sky of dreams,

A tapestry of beasts and struggling men.
Myth is the fleshly act of an invented god:
But not this room where the early sun
Dances in dust, where the overstuffed chair
Squats in a crowded corner, and the piano
Is black and solemn like a household god.

Level in the dreamer's open eye,
A familiar place: chair, room, and chiming clock.
The dreamer waking, feels his own life,
Hears the noise of the life outside,
The shock and bellow of an iron world:
And morning ringing like a great bronze bell,
Swinging in the belfry of a windy sky.

FIGARO TO SUSANNA

The night moves dully in the double bed,
Tossed like a channel crossing; and your head
Bent in the pillow turns despairingly.
    O Susanna, quanta pena mi costi!

Dreams pursue us. The dreadful boojum
Snorts in our traces. Choking gloom and doom
Surround us. Daylight finds us fallow.
    Pace, pace, mio dolce tesoro!

The dim hours of desolation oppress
A glimmering world. All is pain and stress,
Pressure, despair, and infelicity,
    O Susanna, quanta pena mi costi!

An unknown menace in the darkened room
Flutters and flaps. Empty shirt sleeves loom
And beckon, like lost souls blown in sorrow.
    Pace, pace, mio dolce tesoro!

Your hand encloses mine: the tender touch
Of life, the promise made and kept. Of such
Is our dominion, the heart's own sovereignty
Sealed with a love we cannot disallow.
    O Susanna, quanta pena mi costi!
    Pace, pace mio dolce tesoro!

CHILD'S SONG

The sun comes over the cloud: I wake to play
And kick the covers from my squeaking bed.
I hear no other music but the day.

Mother and Father sleep like a load of hay;
The whole house snores: even the chairs are dead:
Why don't they rise or speak or wake to play?

I'm tired of dreams, of what The Stuffed Toys say,
Whether The Wicked Queen is White or Red.
I hear no other music but the day.

Our mouse is small. Why did he run away,
All scratchy feet and whiskery gray head?
If I'm still, will he dance or wake to play?

It's all this sleeping that I mind. I may
Listen at trees for what the squirrel said.
I hear no other music but the day.

The sunlight scatters all the morning gray.
The moon is gone, the nearest star has fled.
My toys are waking and I wake to play.
I hear no other music but the day.

THE JOURNEY TO CASTALIA

—to the memory of Hermann Hesse

It was, from the beginning, a backward journey,
Into the sun's teeth, along a dry road.
Nailed in our skulls, our eyes grew dark with brightness,
Our vision reeled and staggered. We lost our way
In burning meadows clear without shadow,
We lost our way in a wilderness of light.

Only morning and the rising brightness
Were quadrant and compass to this journey.
We crawled under rock and hanging shadow
Where hills climbed to mountains, and the white road
Grew to grass. We walked down in dwindling light,
Groping in darkness, stumbling on the way.

At night we lay suspended in time's shadow:
We watched the stars revolve in pallid brightness,
And talked above the hiss of torchlight.
We dreamed that dawn would end our journey,
That day would end the torment of our way
Endured in sun along a savage road.

Our skins bleached and peeled; our bones dissolved in light.
We cursed and blundered, felt no living shadow;
Then found a line of trees, and there a way
Which moved beyond the edge of blinding brightness.
Our hands together, we regained the road
Unhindered, hurried on our level journey.

Toward a new dominion: where the infirm way
Of marching violence could not cry for light
Or war and pity struggle for the road.
We reached a landscape green with healing shadow,
Concealing gods auspicious for our journey,
A grove of gods who shaded us from brightness.

Reborn in darkness we resumed the road.
No allegoric monsters kept the way,
But animals domestic to our journey
Followed without menace in the light.
We left the sun and came to other brightness:
Music and numbers played in rooms of shadow.

Master of the Journey: we endured the way.
Knew death in blazing light, and life in shadow.
Receive this work against the brightness of the road!

In all climates hear the winds whistle:
Across the plains, sunken in blue snow,
Down from the gray mountains, down to the muddy flats,
Spirals and circles and curves within curves;
Where light flashes from the frozen mud,
Where invisible arrows leap from the bow
Of the icy and bearded north, from
The faceless east,
Points and fronts and dots . . .
Tearing along the ranges and valleys,
Blowing out to the oceans, down the black and turbid rivers,
Matching with lines and shadows the sharpened crescents
And fat-faced, grinning circles of moons,
Always drawing, leading the weather,
Outward to the gathering west,
Turbulent, deepening, tearing the clouds to rain;
And in the green distance, a thin horizon,
Like a solitary thought
Between the headlong earth
And quiet sky
Divides our world from the weather.

VENICE

We walk the stones of Venice. The city
Floats in light. The palaces evoke
The bitten mask, Lord Byron's midnight joke
And tumble in the Grand Canal. Pity
And pride in Byzantine blue and gold.
Shaken in oily waters, the mirrored colors
Streak the green canal. Near St. George a ship
Emerges from a cloud of smoke. We slip
By the grinning boys and money changers,
Reach the *vaporetto* and a crowd
Of German tourists shrieking *Wohl bekannt!*
(We hear of architecture and the dangers
Of Italian food, where the rates are cheap
And the bedsteads large.)

San Marco! We leave the creaking barge.
Two giants beat the bell: the shot of noon.
The pounding hour booms across the square.
A flap and whiz above the long lagoon,
And then the pigeons waddling at our feet.
Once more we board the barge, and find
A cafe in the *Campo Morisimi.*

Coffee and conversation, and we greet
The pleasant doctor with the evil eye.
(Dagger and domino; cinquecento intrigue.
He seemed so strange . . . perhaps he was in league

With you know who!) The pigeons wheel and fly,
Lurch and perch, and moaning flutter down
On this gleaming, most improbable town.

ST. SEBASTIAN

His smile delights the angels in their sphere.
But crowded on the crystal rim of heaven
Principality and Power cannot bear
To watch the insolent tall bowmen
Notch their arrows. Transfigured and transfixed,
Posed in tranquility, he wears the mixed
Distinctions of his doom: his future peace,
His present pain.
                              He turns away from pain:
The steel bolts trembling in his groin and brain.
Calmness of heart. Neither suffering nor growing
To desired glory. Only knowing.
In That Will, his resurrection and release.

THE COURTESAN

—after Rilke

The sun of Venice burns my hair
To gold: transformed by flaming alchemy.
Beneath my charcoaled brows the changing sea
Mirrors the silent peril of my eye,

Sold for a bargain on the water where
Shylock in merry sport exacted flesh
For money. With shining bait I fish
For fools who flounder in my mesh.

One pets my dog. Another's finger grips
My unresisting hand, relaxed in gold
And jewelled fire: invulnerable and cold.

My bed invites the world and on my lips
The green hopes of ancient families lie—
Taste the venom of my mouth, and die.

PARSIFAL

My mother told me not to speak unless
Spoken to. Can I know or guess
This wizard's riddling: a white lance
Bleeding red, a rusted sword thrust
In my hands? The fisherman's glance
And grief distract me as they bring
Another wondrous Thing,
Grimed with rotten food and dust:
A dish that feeds this crowd
Of howlers. . . .
                I see the unplowed
Fields crumble in the summer sun. And the day
Drops. In this chamber, wild with dreams,
I fight great kings beneath a tapestry
Of woven battle. Gray and gray and gray
The morning grips my sleep. I flee
This house, this land held outright by the crow.
I stumble into light.
              I do not know. . . .

THE RENUNCIATION

Now that I have given all that up, and I
ride so easy in my ill-gotten virtue,
smug as any pasty fool, I tell over
my beads, remembering in my orisons
that persistent nymph who haunted my blank days,
my green nights tangled in one recurring dream:

I stand amazed, held in a wizard spell
(a magic black as that filthy kitchen, where
old Faust regained his lust), chained in every bone.
I watch from a tower of self-possession
the dotted eyebeams leap across the landscape
and my coward shadow flees the stalking sun.

Now that I have given all that up, I know
that daylight will rout me from my bed, and I,
purged of my bilious humor, will bravely face
what wicked men contrive or the gods ordain.
Yet I shall remember her arms were slender,
the grass not bent where her brown body had lain.

BRITH

By winged Dominions
And flaming Powers,
(Who guard the Ark
And Heaven's towers),

You are bound to Elohim
In blood, in blood;
Your cry to Him
Is understood.

The Law is sharper
Than the knife:
O child receive
The wound of life.

AUBADE

1

Sleepers and countrymen, reach me my ears!
Deep in sound I lie, merely alive and
Music around me wells to the unwelcome day.
Squealing like bagpipes, our children
Serenade God and all the tender angels.

2

Common, uncommon. This is no joking matter:
I am dim until the light takes hold.
Morning opens like a new-hung door; sleep
Unclasps me and I come to, stiff in every joint,
Tangle and convolution, limb and thought.

I ascend like a diver to meet the day.

3

Our children's days are still their own; they walk
A world of hilarious games, across a floor
Splendid with sunlight. In mornings of love
They greet the household like travelers
Returned from a journey: waking their toys,
Shaking us from sleep with such glad cries.

SHADRACH: Bound in hat and hose
And linen coat,
I walk in fire by the king's decree.
No smell of fire upon me:
(Though in flame I float)
No smell but myrrh and attar of rose.

MESHACH: The brassy furnace glows.
I hold high talk
With the angel of our mystery.
No smell of fire upon me:
(Though in flame I walk)
No smell but myrrh and attar of rose.

ABED-NEGO: Seven times the heat grows,
But cannot burn,
His shadow is cool as God's own tree.
No smell of fire upon me:
(Though in flame I turn)
No smell but myrrh and attar of rose.

JET

Across the cloud
Pointed with light
Darts the tongue
Of the roaring plane

Earth explodes
Under its fire
Searing the stone
Consuming the air

No hawk, no Harpy
Disputes its place
Poised at the sun
At the heart of life

The enemy is ill-defined. He skulks
In shadows, trades in vile transaction,
Lurks and beckons. Doppelgängers glimmer,
Grins and scowls fade in the foggy air.
Beyond the ruined park and giant wheel
The lilac tree and chestnut blossom.
Voices leap and fall; the language chokes:
The cataleptic speech of Doctor Crud
Enforces faith; the words of Bishop Skin
Reduce our sins to platitudes. Believe
The rusted General in rotten armor,
Marvelous ill-favored, smiling. Believe
This woman, long in lust: hear O hear
This strumpet of a sophistry. Recant
The heresy of private love; betray
Your friends in coils of intricate deceit;
Lose honor in corruption, and learn
The empty answers to reactionary evil:
The blank terms of liberal abstraction.

Belief is unrestrained beyond belief.

ON THE EASTERN FRONT

—*after Georg Trakl*

Like the wild organ of a winter storm
The black wrath of groaning troops,
The crimson surge of slaughter,
Defoliate stars.

Night beckons dying soldiers, shattered heads,
And silver glint of arms.
The ash-tree of autumn shadows
Sighing ghosts.

Thorny wasteland strangles the city.
From bloody steps
The moon hunts terrified women.

Wild wolves broke through the door.

WAR IN HEAVEN

A wind stirs up the demon of this night.
I creep to comfort in a deeper dream,
And meet a man who heard the muses scream,
Who touched the flint and iron of his mind
And read Kaballa by that crackling light.

Who saw dead lovers couple in midair;
Who saw God's startled Mother turn and stare
To see the bright dove flutter, and to find
The world appalled by what her heart had fed.

He hangs above the weather and looks down
Upon the living and the nearly dead
Where a host of weeping angels stand,
Helpless with their flameless swords to stop
The outbreak of the gods above our land.

GRODEK

—after Georg Trakl

At evening the autumn woods echo
With murderous weapons, echo the golden plains,
The blue lakes; and over all the sun
Descends to darkness. The night embraces
Warriors dying, the savage cries
Of their broken mouths.
And quietly gathering in the meadowland
A crimson cloud: within lives an angry god,
The spilt blood—cold as the moon.

All streets dissolve in black corruption.

Beneath the golden branches of night and stars,
The Sister's shadow stirs through the quiet willow leaves,
Greeting the ghosts of heroes, the bleeding heads;
And lightly the dark flutes of autumn resound in the reeds.
O stiff-necked grief! You brazen altars,
The spirit's blazing flame nourishes a dominion of pain:
Our children's children yet unborn.

LENINGRAD, 1937

—from the memoirs of Anna Akhmatova

On the darkest night of the shortest day,
He came without money. Lights flickered
High in blackness; in soot and steel
Snow leaked through the station roof.

He came without money, without clothes.
Disaster sat in cafes; drunken officials
Signed blank forms of death:
Many had already disappeared.

He sickened in dreams, straining to hear
The gathering silence. His breath came heavy,
His lips caught air. We talked of books,
But telephones kept ringing, doors hung open.

It was no time to talk of books.

AUTUMN VALEDICTION

I

Begin the phrase in deepest tones.
Above the bass, the oboe's amber voice
Pleading the songs of autumn,

The *Ewigkeit* of lonely afternoons
And ghosts who flit from hedge to hill,
Moaning like madmen, wandering without torch,

Wandering, waiting. Music can say this
In eloquent violence. Between the strings and horns
We come direct and unadorned, feeling

The luminous brain: that fiery excellence
Alone the nerves, outshining night,
The darkness of what we think we know.

II

In these fires I have read the hornbook of night:
Its crotchets and quavers dancing down the page,
Down the spaces between the enormous stars,

And known that music is the abstract agony.
Not the sound alone that pierces all our sense,
Or point for point in counterpoint.

But the form of love, the body of time.
A midnight pomp dark in black and gold,
Moving our grief with unshed tears; or love

Where we become her trembling heart and shame;
His virile cries. The image breaks, dissolves
In words, words, words. The rest is Mozart.

III
The sensual circle tightens; the ache
Deepens as once again the days turn cold,
And I remember luncheons on the grass,

The weekend voyages to Cytherea,
The flesh of generous girls
Undressing where the low-voiced streams unwind.

The phrase descends in silver sharps and flats:
Ewig . . . ewig . . . ewig . . .
Turning a long slow trill against the strings,

Against the dying flutes and horns,
Against the weather and the falling of the leaves,
Against this man, dreaming beyond his dream.

Even this landscape is ambiguous. Purple moors
Slide down to Italianate beaches,
Desert winds blow across the mountains,
Across the yellow distance
Between the cities of the plain
And the cities of the shore.

                         Golden boys and girls
Stride in tranquil grace; Artemis and Apollo
Ease along the asphalt roads to the white beaches.
The ocean swirls around the depredation
Of gimcrack houses perched on faulted land,
And the air hovers like Geryon
Over foul highways panting in the sun.

No prophet has been equal to the place.
Those who survive succumb.
Those who came to rage
Stay to enjoy the weather,
Submit to the imperative of perpetual sex,
Or simply make money.

I dream of Knossos and Carthage,
Naples under mythical skies, unrepentant Pompeii
Beneath the fire of the outraged gods,

Atlantis crumbling to the watery floor.

PLANS FOR AN ORDERLY APOCALYPSE

The sirens sang when the heavens split
The day dawned dark when the town was taken
The streets were still and the people gone
And grass had grown where the stone was cracked

The skies blazed black with melting steel
Airmen in armor swung down on silk
Drowned submarines expired in sand
In flash of fission the Phoenix fell

The church door burst in a marble blast
Scorched angels flew from the flaming crypts
Stinking of feathers and singèd hair
I thought of the Prince and his pitchforked crew

But the King and Queen stayed late in bed
Matted in love and matters of state
The princess cried when her cradle cracked
Nurse was dead and nobody heard

In the pantry the cook and the butler kissed
Smelling of pie and turnips and tea
Down in the orchard, tumbled in apples
The rational gardener gasped his end

The Pullman Porter pulled his bell
"All out, all out, for Armageddon"
Liberal laughter sneered at his doom
And the Whites and the Reds trooped to their tomb